The Summers

first reader

Maud Summers

Alpha Editions

This edition published in 2024

ISBN : 9789364738804

Design and Setting By
Alpha Editions
www.alphaedis.com
Email - info@alphaedis.com

As per information held with us this book is in Public Domain.
This book is a reproduction of an important historical work. Alpha Editions uses the best technology to reproduce historical work in the same manner it was first published to preserve its original nature. Any marks or number seen are left intentionally to preserve its true form.

THE LITTLE RED APPLE.

Once there was a little red apple.
It was high up in a tree.
A little girl saw the apple.
"Oh, Apple!" she said. "Come down to me."
But the little red apple did not hear her, for it was fast asleep.
The bright sun came out.
"Oh, Sun! Dear Sun!" said the little girl. "Will you waken the apple?"
The sun kissed the apple, but it did not fall down.
A little bird sat upon the bough of a tree.
"Little Bird, can you waken the apple?"
The bird sang a pretty song, but that did not waken the apple.
"Here comes West Wind," said the little girl.
"He will waken the apple for me."
West Wind shook the tree and down fell the apple.
"Thank you, West Wind," said the little girl.

The north wind doth blow,
And we shall have snow,
And what will the robin do then?
  Poor thing!
He 'll sit in a barn,
And keep himself warm,
And hide his head under his wing,
  Poor thing!

The north wind doth blow,
And we shall have snow,
And what will the robin do then?
Poor thing!

He'll sit in a barn,
And keep himself warm,
And hide his head under his wing,
Poor thing!

THE WIND AND THE SUN.

One day West Wind blew the tops of the trees.
He blew the corn in the fields.
He blew the apples off the trees.
Just then the bright sun came out.
"I am stronger than you," said West Wind.
"No! I am stronger than you," said the sun.
Then West Wind said, "Do you see that man?
He has on a warm coat.
I can make the man take it off."
"Can you?" said the sun.
West Wind blew, and blew, and blew.
But the man did not take off his coat.
"This is a cold wind," he said.

"Now it is my turn," said the sun.
"I can make the man take off his coat."
"Do it," said West Wind.
The sun came out very hot.
Soon the man took off his coat.
"The sun is very hot," he said.

THE WIND.

Who has seen the wind?
Neither I nor you;
But when the leaves hang trembling
The wind is passing through.

Who has seen the wind?
Neither you nor I;
But when the trees bow down their heads
The wind is passing by.
CHRISTINA G. ROSSETTI.

SOMETHING TO TELL.

Who has seen the wind?
Who can sing the wind song?
When do the leaves hang trembling?
When do the trees bow their heads?
What work does North Wind do?
What work does South Wind do?
What work does East Wind do?
What work does West Wind do?

What does the sun do in spring?
What does the sun do in summer?
What does the sun do in autumn?
What does the sun do in winter?
Did the sun make the apple fall?
Did the wind make the man take off his coat?
Is the sun stronger than the wind?

MOTHER TREE AND THE LEAVES.

One day Mother Tree said to the leaf-buds,
"Winter will soon be here.
I have made you warm winter coats."

Mother Tree put a coat around every leaf-bud.

"Sunshine will keep you warm," she said.
"So I have put some sunshine in every coat."

Soon all the leaf-buds went to sleep
for the winter.

Then Mother Tree said to the little green leaves,
"Now your work is over.
Take off your green dresses.
Jack Frost will be here to-night.
He will give you bright red and yellow dresses."

II

In the morning Mother Tree said,
"Waken, dear leaves.
It is time to get up.
See! Here are red and yellow dresses for you.
Now you may fly away to play in the brown fields."
Just then North Wind passed by.
He saw the leaves hang trembling on Mother Tree.
"Come!" said North Wind.
"Come with me."
"Goodby, dear Mother Tree," said the leaves as they flew away.
Over the brown fields they went with North Wind.
All day they danced and sang in the brown fields.
When night came they went to sleep.

Soon they were covered with the soft white snow.

THE LITTLE PINE TREE.

Once there was a little pine tree.
It had long green needles.
"I wish I had leaves," said the pine tree.
"I do not like needles.
I should like leaves of gold."
By and by night came.
The little pine tree went to sleep.

II

In the morning the pine tree had leaves of gold.
"How happy I am!" said the pine tree.
"See what pretty leaves I have!"
Soon a man came into the woods.
He put all the gold leaves into a bag.

Then the poor tree had no leaves.
"Oh! What shall I do?" said the tree.
"I do not like gold leaves.
I wish I had leaves of glass."

Again it was night.
The little pine tree went to sleep.

III

In the morning the tree had leaves of glass.
"Now I am happy," said the pine tree.
Just then the wind blew the tree.
It blew all the leaves off the tree.
They fell down and were broken.
"Oh! My pretty glass leaves," said the poor tree.
"See! They are all broken.
I do not like leaves of glass.
I wish I had green leaves."
Again night came.
The little pine tree went to sleep.

IV

In the morning the tree had pretty green leaves.
"I am happy now," said the pine tree.
"I have green leaves like the other trees."
By and by a little goat came into the woods.
Soon the goat ate all the leaves off the tree.
Poor little pine tree!
Again it had no leaves.
"I wish I had my long green needles," said the tree.
"How happy I should be with needles!"
Night came.
Again the pine tree went to sleep.

V

In the morning it had long green needles.
The pine tree was very happy.
Two little birds flew into the tree.
They made a nest in the long green needles.
"I will never wish for leaves again," said the pine tree.
"A man took my gold leaves.
The wind broke my glass leaves.
A goat ate my green leaves.
Needles are best for a little pine tree."

THE ANT AND THE DOVE.

A little ant fell into the water.
"Oh, help! Help!" said the ant.
A dove was in a tree near by.
She dropped a leaf into the water.
"Here, little ant, is a leaf.
Climb upon it," said the dove.
Soon the ant came to the shore.
"Thank you, pretty dove," said the ant
"Some day I will help you."

II

One day the dove was in a tree near her nest
A man came into the woods with a gun.
He tried to shoot the dove.
The ant passed by and saw him.
"Oh, the poor dove!" said the ant.
"How can I help her?"
She ran to the man and bit his foot.
"Oh, my foot! My foot!" said the man.
Then he ran out of the woods.
"Thank you," said the dove.
"You have helped me, little friend."

STOP, STOP, PRETTY WATER!

"Stop, stop, pretty water!"
Said Mary one day,
To a bright, happy brook
That was running away.

"You run on so fast!
I wish you would stay;
My boat and my flowers
You will carry away.

But I will run after:
Mother says that I may;
For I would know where
You are running away."

So Mary ran on;
But I have heard say,
That she never could find
Where the brook ran away.
ELIZA LEE FOLLEN.

THE BROOK.

One day some raindrops fell out of the sky.
They went running down a hillside.
By and by they came to a bright, happy brook.
"Stop, stop, pretty water!" said the raindrops.
"Where are you going?"
"I am going to the sea," said the brook.
"I can not stop. I have work to do.
I water the grass and the flowers.
The cows come here to drink.
I make a home for the fishes.
The birds like my pure cold water.
The boys and the girls come here to play.

There are other little brooks.
They all go my way, so we run on together."
"We will go with you, too," said the raindrops.
So away they went with the bright, happy brook.

THE THREE BEARS.

One day Golden Locks went into the woods.
She came to a little house.
It was the home of three bears.
Father Bear was a big bear.
Mother Bear was a middle-sized bear.
Baby Bear was a little bear.
The three bears were not at home.
So Golden Locks went into the house.

II

Golden Locks saw three bowls of milk.
There was a big bowl.
That was for Father Bear.
There was a middle-sized bowl.
That was for Mother Bear.
There was a little bowl.
That was for Baby Bear.
She tasted the milk in the big bowl.
It was too hot.
She tasted the milk in the middle-sized bowl.
It was too cold.
She tasted the milk in the little bowl.
It was just right.
So she drank all of it.

III

Golden Locks saw three chairs.
There was a big chair.
That was for Father Bear.
There was a middle-sized chair.
That was for Mother Bear.
There was a little chair.
That was for Baby Bear.
She sat in the big chair.
It was too hard.
She sat in the middle-sized chair.
It was too soft.
She sat in the little chair.
But the little chair broke, and Golden Locks fell down.

IV

Then Golden Locks saw three beds.
There was a big bed.
That was for Father Bear.
There was a middle-sized bed.
That was for Mother Bear.
There was a little bed.
That was for Baby Bear.
She lay down on the big bed.
It was too hard.

She lay down on the middle-sized bed.
It was too soft.
She lay down on the little bed.
It was just right.
So she fell fast asleep.

V

Soon the three bears came home.
Father Bear said, in a big voice,
"SOME ONE HAS BEEN TASTING MY MILK."
Mother Bear said, in a voice not so big,
"SOME ONE HAS BEEN TASTING MY MILK."
Baby Bear said, in a little voice,
"SOME ONE HAS BEEN TASTING MY MILK, AND IT IS ALL GONE."

VI

Then Father Bear said, in a big voice,
"SOME ONE HAS BEEN SITTING IN MY CHAIR."
Mother Bear said, in a voice not so big,

"SOME ONE HAS BEEN SITTING IN MY CHAIR."
Baby Bear said, in a little voice,
"SOME ONE HAS BEEN SITTING IN MY CHAIR, AND HAS BROKEN IT."

VII

Then Father Bear said, in a big voice,
"SOME ONE HAS BEEN LYING ON MY BED."
Mother Bear said, in a voice not so big,
"SOME ONE HAS BEEN LYING ON MY BED."
Baby Bear said, in a little voice,
"SOME ONE HAS BEEN LYING ON MY BED, HERE SHE IS, FAST ASLEEP."

VIII

Just then Golden Locks sat up in bed.
She saw the three bears looking at her.
She jumped off the bed.
Then she ran out of the house.
She ran home as fast as she could.

THE FOX AND THE CROW.

One day a crow flew into a tree.
She had some cheese.
Just then a fox came along.
"I must have that cheese," said the fox.
He looked up at the crow and said,
"How pretty you are!
Can you sing, pretty bird?"
The crow sang, "Caw! Caw! Caw!"
Down fell the cheese.
Then the fox ran off with it.

CHICKEN LITTLE.

One day Chicken Little was in the woods.
A nut fell on her head.
"Oh, oh! The sky is falling," said Chicken Little,
"I must run and tell the king."
So she ran, and she ran.
On the way she met Henny Penny.

II

"Where are you going?" said Henny Penny.
"The sky is falling," said Chicken Little.
"I am going to tell the king."

"I will go with you," said Henny Penny.
So Chicken Little and Henny Penny ran, and ran, and ran.
At last they met Cocky Locky.

III

"Where are you going?" said Cocky Locky.
"Oh, oh! The sky is falling," they said.
"We are going to tell the king."
"I will go with you," said Cocky Locky.
So Chicken Little and Henny Penny and Cocky Locky ran and ran.
When they came to some water, they saw Ducky Lucky.

IV

"Where are you going?" said Ducky Lucky.
"The sky is falling," they said.
"We are going to tell the king."
"I will go with you," said Ducky Lucky. "We must run fast."
So Chicken Little, Henny Penny, Cocky Locky and Ducky Lucky ran, and ran.
At the top of the hill they met Turkey Lurkey.

V

"Where are you going?" said Turkey Lurkey.
"The sky is falling," they said.
"We are going to tell the king."
"I will go with you," said Turkey Lurkey.

So Chicken Little, Henny Penny, Cocky Locky, Ducky Lucky, and Turkey Lurkey, ran down the hill.

Foxy Loxy heard them and ran out of his den.

VI

"Where are you going?" said Foxy Loxy.
"Oh, oh! The sky is falling," they said.
"We are going to tell the king."
"Come with me," said Foxy Loxy.
"I will take you to the king."
So Chicken Little, Henny Penny, Cocky Locky, Ducky Lucky, and Turkey Lurkey, went with Foxy Loxy.
He took them into his den, and they never saw the king.

THE SWING.

How do you like to go up in a swing,
Up in the air so blue?
Oh, I do think it the pleasantest thing
Ever a child can do!

Up in the air and over the wall,
Till I can see so wide,
Rivers and trees and cattle and all
Over the countryside—

Till I look down on the garden green,
Down on the roof so brown—
Up in the air I go flying again,
Up in the air and down!
ROBERT LOUIS STEVENSON.

THE KIND OLD OAK.

It was time for winter to come.
There was no green grass in the fields.
The birds were all in the South.
Under an old oak-tree, there were some sweet blue violets.
"Dear oak-tree," said they.
"Winter will soon be here.
We are afraid of the cold."
"Do not be afraid, pretty violets," said the oak.
"Go to sleep, I will take care of you."
So the violets went to sleep.
The kind old tree dropped a red leaf upon them.
Then leaf after leaf dropped down.
Soon the violets were all covered over.
Winter came but they were not afraid.
They were fast asleep under the leaves of the kind old oak.

IN THE WOODS.

Here are some woodmen.
They are in the deep woods.
Two woodmen are cutting down a tree.
How fast they work!
See the ax go up and down.
Soon the tree will fall.
See! Down it comes!
Other woodmen cut off the boughs.
Then they cut the tree into logs.
By and by they will take the logs to the water.
They will put the logs on the ice.
In the spring the warm sunshine will melt the ice.
Then the water will carry the logs down to the sawmill.

THE HONEST WOODMAN.

A woodman was at work near the water.
He was cutting down a large oak-tree.
You could hear the chip, chip, chip of his ax.
He lifted the ax high over his head to give a good blow.
The ax fell into the water.
The poor woodman looked down into the deep water.
He said, "Oh! What shall I do?
I have lost my good ax!"

II

A kind fairy lived in the water.
She came up out of the water and said,
"My poor man, why are you crying?"
"Oh! said the woodman.
"I have lost my good ax."
"Do not cry," said the fairy.
"I will get your ax for you."
The fairy went down into the deep water.
Soon she came up with a gold ax.
"Is this your ax?" said the fairy.
"Oh, no!" said the
"That is not my ax."
The fairy again went down into the water.
Soon she came up with a silver ax.
"Is this your ax?" she said.
"Oh, no, no!" said the woodman.
"That is not my old ax."

III

Then the fairy said, "You shall have your ax."
She went down into the water again.
Soon she came up with a steel ax.

"Oh, thank you!" said the happy woodman. "That is my ax.
Now I can work."
"Yes," said the fairy, "this is your ax, but it is a steel ax.
Did you not like the gold ax and the silver ax?"
"This is my ax," said the woodman.
"The gold ax was not mine, and the silver ax was not mine."
"You are an honest woodman," said the fairy.
"You would take only what is yours.
So I will give you the gold ax
and the silver ax."
The woodman carried home the gold ax, the silver ax and the steel ax.
He was very, very happy.

AN OLD RHYME.

If all the seas were one sea,
What a great sea that would be!
If all the trees were one tree,
What a great tree that would be!
If all the axes were one ax,
What a great ax that would be!
If all the men were one man,
What a great man that would be!
And if the great man took the great ax,
And cut down the great tree,
And let it fall into the great sea,
What a great splash that would be!

AT THE SEASIDE.

When I was down beside the sea
A wooden spade they gave to me
To dig the sandy shore.
My holes were empty like a cup,
In every hole the sea came up,
Till it could come no more.
ROBERT LOUIS STEVENSON

LITTLE RED RIDING HOOD.

Once upon a time there was a pretty little girl.
Her grandmother made her a pretty red hood.
Then everyone called her Little Red Riding Hood.
One day her mother made some butter and a cake.
She put these into a basket and said, "Your grandmother is sick, Little Red Riding Hood.
Will you take this cake and butter to her?"
"Oh, yes, Mother!" said Little Red Riding Hood.
"I know the way to Grandmother's house."
She put on her red hood and kissed her mother.
"Good-by, Little Red Riding Hood," said her mother.
"Be a good girl and do not go out of the path."

II

Little Red Riding Hood sang as she went along.
When she came to the wood she met a wolf.
Some woodmen were at work near by.
The wolf was afraid of the woodmen.
So he said to Red Riding Hood,
"Good morning, little girl.
Where are you going?"

"I am going to see my grandmother," said Little Red Riding Hood.
"I have butter and a cake for her."
"Where does your grandmother live?" said the wolf.
"She lives on the other side of the wood," said Little Red Riding Hood.
"The house is near three big trees."
"I will go to see your grandmother, too," said the wolf.
He went beside Red Riding Hood for a little way.
Then the wolf said, "Little Red Riding Hood, see the pretty flowers all around us.
Why do you not pick some of them?"
"Grandmother loves flowers," said Little Red Riding Hood.
"I will pick some to put in the basket with the cake and butter."
So Little Red Riding Hood went out of the path to look for flowers.
But the wolf ran through the wood as fast as he could go.
He saw the grandmother's house near three big oak trees.

III

The wolf ran to the house.
He knocked at the grandmother's door, "Tap, tap, tap!"
No one came to the door.
He went into the house and looked all around.
The grandmother was not at home.
"Oh," said the wolf, "I know what I will do!"
He put the grandmother's cap on his head.
Then he lay down and covered himself with the bed-clothes.
By and by Little Red Riding Hood came to her grandmother's house.
She knocked at the door,
"Tap, tap, tap!"
"Who is there?" said the wolf in a soft voice.
"It is I, Little Red Riding Hood."
"Come in," said the wolf.
"Good morning, Grandmother," said Little Red Riding Hood.
"I have butter and a cake for you.
Mother put them in my basket."

"Put down your basket and come here, my dear," said the wolf.
Little Red Riding Hood went to the bed.

IV

"Oh, Grandmother, what big eyes you have!"
"The better to see you, my dear.
"What long ears you have, Grandmother!"
"The better to hear you, my dear."
"What long arms you have, Grandmother!"
"The better to hug you, my dear."
"Oh, Grandmother, what big teeth you have!"
"The better to eat you, my dear."
But just then the woodmen came in.
The grandmother was with them.
The woodmen killed the wolf.
Then they took Little Red Riding Hood home.
When Little Red Riding Hood saw her mother she said,
"Oh, Mother! I will never go out of the path again."

THE SONG OF THE MILL-STREAM.

"Turn!" said the little stream.
"Turn! O turn! Turn! O turn!"
"Turn!" said the little stream
As it pushed against the wheel.
"I push, you know, to help you go,
To saw the logs and boards."
MILDRED AND PATTY HILL (*Adapted*).

THE SAWMILL.

Zish! Zish! Zish! Hear the sawmill!
There it is by the water.
See the wheel go round and round.
Splash! Splash! Splash!
Hear the water!
It falls upon the wheel and turns it around.
Around and around goes the big mill wheel.
Buzz! Buzz! Buzz!
What a busy sawmill!
All day long it saws the logs into boards.
Here are boards to make houses and barns.
Here are boards to make beds and chairs.
Here are boards to make playthings for girls and boys.
Work! Work! Work! All the day long!
Oh, see what good work the sawmill can do!

THE LION AND THE MOUSE.

One day a big lion was asleep in the woods.
A mouse ran over the lion's paw.
The big lion caught the little mouse.
"Oh, Lion!" said the mouse.
"Let me go. Please let me go.
Some day I will help you."
"How can you help me?" said the lion.
"You are too little to help a big lion."
But he lifted his paw and away the mouse ran.

II

Some time after this the lion was in the woods.
He was caught in a net.
He could not get out.
Just then the little mouse passed by.
"Oh, the poor lion!" said the mouse.
"How can I help him?"
She ran to the lion and said,
"Kind friend, I will help you."
The mouse cut the net with her sharp teeth.
"Thank you," said the lion.
"I see that a mouse can help a lion."

THE THREE LITTLE PIGS.

A mother pig had three little pigs.
Browny was a dirty pig. He liked to roll in the mud.
Whitey was a greedy pig. She would eat and eat and then cry for more.
Blacky was a good pig. He was bright and happy all day long.

II

One day the mother pig called the three pigs to her and said,
"Browny! What kind of a house would you like?"
"I should like to have a mud house,
Mother dear," said Browny.

"And you, Whitey! What kind of a house shall I make for you?" said the mother.
"Oh, I should like a great big cabbage house, Mother!" said Whitey.
"Blacky dear! What kind of a house would you like?" said the mother pig.
"A brick house, please, Mother," said Blacky.
So the good mother pig made three houses.
Then the three little pigs went to live in them.
As they were going away the mother pig said, "If Mr. Fox comes to see you, do not let him in. He is not a friend."

III

Browny was very happy in his mud house.
One day there came a "Tap, tap!" at the door.
A soft voice said, "Little pig!
Little pig! Let me come in."
"Who are you?" said Browny.
"I am a friend of your mother's," said the soft voice.
"I want to see your pretty house."
"Oh, no!" said Browny. "You are not a friend. You are Mr. Fox.
You can not come in."
Then Mr. Fox made a hole in the mud house.
He put Browny into a bag and carried him away to his den.

IV

The next day the old fox went to Whitey's house.
Greedy little Whitey was eating the cabbage that her house was made of.
"Tap, tap!" came a knock at the door.
Then a soft voice said, "Little pig!
Little pig! Let me come in."
"Who are you?" said Whitey.
"A friend of your mother's," said Mr. Fox.
"I have something good for you to eat."
"No, no! You can not come in.
You are not a friend," said Whitey.
Then Mr. Fox ate a big hole in the cabbage house.

He put Whitey into a bag and carried her to his den.

V

The next day the fox went to Blacky's house.
"Tap, tap!" came a knock at the door.
"Little pig! Little pig! Let me come in," said a soft voice.
"Who are you?" said Blacky.
"I am a friend of your mother's," said Mr. Fox.
"Oh, no! You are not," said Blacky.
"You can not come in.
You carried away Whitey and Browny. You are not going to get me."
Then Mr. Fox tried to knock down the house.
But he could not get into Blacky's strong brick house.

VI

The next day Blacky went to town to get a big kettle.
As he came back he saw Mr. Fox in the woods.
"Oh, what shall I do!" said Blacky.
He had just come to the top of a hill.
At the foot of the hill he could see his strong brick house.
Blacky got into the kettle.
It rolled over and over down the hill.
At the door of the brick house
Blacky jumped out.

VII

Blacky ran into the house as fast as he could go.
He put the kettle full of water over the fire.
Mr. Fox was afraid when he saw the big black kettle rolling down the hill.
When he saw Blacky jump out of the kettle he said,
"O ho! I will have you now."
He ran down to Blacky's house.
He tried the door but he could not get in.
Then he went down the chimney.
He fell into the kettle of hot water.
Then Blacky went to get Whitey and Browny.
Mr. Fox had carried them to his den in the woods.
After that they all lived together in Blacky's strong brick house.

THE BOY AND THE NUTS.

Once there was a greedy little boy.
He saw some nuts in a pitcher.
He put his hand into the pitcher.
"I will take a big handful," he said.
But he could not take out the handful of nuts.
He did not wish to drop the nuts.
At last he began to cry.
Just then his mother came into the room.
"Why are you crying?" she said.
"I can not take this handful of nuts out of the pitcher."
"Take one nut," said his mother.
"Then you can get your hand out."

THE NEW MOON.

Dear mother, how pretty
The moon looks to-night!
She was never so pretty before.

Her two little horns
Are so sharp and so bright—
I hope she'll not grow any more.

If I were up there,
With you and my friends,
I'd rock in it nicely, you see;

I'd sit in the middle,
And hold by both ends.
Oh, what a bright cradle 't would be!

And there we would stay
In the beautiful skies,
And through the bright clouds we would roam.

We would see the sun set
And see the sun rise,
And, on the next rainbow, come home.
ELIZA LEE FOLLEN.

THE CARPENTER.

"Good morning, Mr. Carpenter.
May I come in?
See, I have broken my sled.
Can you mend it for me?"
"Yes, I can mend it," said the carpenter.
"Here is a board but it is too long."
"Buzz! Buzz! Buzz!" sang the saw.
"Now I must plane it," said the carpenter.
"Zish! Zish! Zish!" said the plane.
"This board is just right," said the carpenter.
"Rap-a-tap, tap!" said the hammer.
As the carpenter works he sings this song,
"Rap-a-tap, tap! Tick-a-tack, too!
Here is your sled as good as new."
"Thank you, Mr. Carpenter.
When I am a man I should like to be a carpenter, too."

SOMETHING TO TELL.

Where do we get wood?
How is wood used?
Find something in this room made of wood.
Who cuts down the trees?
How do the logs get down to the sawmill?
What do the men in the sawmill do?
Who has seen a carpenter at work?
Can you name the carpenter's tools?
Tell me something a carpenter makes.
Find something made with a hammer.
Find something made with a plane.
Find something made with a saw.
What tools have you?
What will you be when you are a man?

THE GINGERBREAD BOY.

A little old man and a little old woman lived together in a little old house.
The little old house was near a deep wood.
One morning the little old woman was baking gingerbread cakes.
She cut out some round gingerbread cakes.
Then she said to the little old man,
"See! I have cut out a cake to look just like a little boy."
Then she put The Gingerbread Boy in the oven to bake.
Not long after the little old woman went to the oven to look at her cake.
Out jumped The Gingerbread Boy.
Away he ran as fast as he could go.
The little old woman and the little old man ran after him, but they could not catch him.

II

The Gingerbread Boy ran on and on.
At last he came to a barn full of threshers.
As he went by the door he said,
"I have run away from
A little old woman,
A little old man,
And I can run away from you,
I can, I can."
Then the threshers ran after him, but they could not catch him.
The Gingerbread Boy ran on and on.
Soon he came to a field full of mowers.
As he passed the field he called out,
"I have run away from
A little old woman,
A little old man,
A barn full of threshers,
And I can run away from you, I can, I can."
Then the mowers ran after him, but they could not catch him.

III

The Gingerbread Boy ran on and on, till he came to a cow.
He called out to the cow,

"I have run away from
A little old woman,
A little old man,
A barn full of threshers,
A field full of mowers,
And I can run away from you,
I can, I can."
Then the cow ran after him, but she could not catch him.
The Gingerbread Boy ran on and on
Soon he met a fox and called out, "I have run away from
A little old woman,
A little old man,

A barn full of threshers,
A field full of mowers,
A cow,
And I can run away from you,

I can, I can."
Then the fox ran after him.

IV

Now a fox can run very fast.
On and on ran the fox until he caught The Gingerbread Boy.
Then the fox began to eat him.
"Dear me!" said The Gingerbread Boy
"Here I am a quarter gone.
Now I am half gone.
I am three-quarters gone.
Oh, dear! I am all gone."
And he never spoke again.

THE CITY MOUSE AND THE COUNTRY MOUSE.

One day a city mouse went to visit a country mouse.
The country mouse lived in a field.
The two mice ran about the field and had a happy time.
At last the country mouse said,
"We must have something to eat."
He gave the city mouse an ear of corn.
This was enough for the country mouse.
But the city mouse did not like it.
So he said to the country mouse,
"My friend! Is this all you have to eat?
Come to the city and visit me.
I live in a beautiful house.
Come and see what good things
I have to eat."
So the two mice set off for the city.

II

After a while they came to the house where the city mouse lived.
Oh! What good things the city mouse set before the country mouse!
She had bread and cheese and cake.
"How good this is!" said the country mouse.
"I wish I lived in the city."

Just then a man came into the room.
The mice jumped down and ran into a hole.
"Do not be afraid," said the city mouse.
"The man can not find us."
By and by the man went away.

Then the mice ran out of the hole and again began to eat.

III

Soon a cat came into the room.
"The cat! The cat!" said the city mouse.
Away ran the mice as fast as they could go.
Poor little country mouse!
She said to the city mouse,
"Good-by, my friend, I am going home.
In the country I am not afraid.
You have a beautiful house and good things to eat.
But I like my corn better than your cake."

THE CITY MOUSE AND THE GARDEN MOUSE.

The city mouse lives in a house;
The garden mouse lives in a bower;
He's friendly with the frogs and toads,
And sees the pretty plants in flower.
The city mouse eats bread and cheese;
The garden mouse eats what he can;
We will not grudge him seeds and stalks,
Poor little timid, furry man.
CHRISTIANA G. ROSSETTI.

THE MINER.

Here is a miner at work.
He is away down in a deep coal mine.
The sun does not shine in the dark coal mine.
So the miner has a little lamp in his cap.
Now he can see the hard, black coal.
See him lift his pick ax.
Click, click, click-ity click!
Hear the song of the pick ax!
He digs out the coal with his sharp pick.
All day long the busy miner is at work.
At night he comes out of the dark coal mine.
He gets into a strong iron basket.
Then he goes up, up, up, out of the mine.
How happy he must be to see the bright sunshine!

THE ENGINE.

"Puff, puff, puff!" Hear the engine!
It runs through field and wood.
It runs through the country and the city.
"Puff, puff, puff!" See the long train.
The cars are full of coal.
They have come from the coal mine.
Next winter we shall be warm and happy beside the fire.
Then we shall think of the busy miner down in the dark mine.
"Puff, puff, puff!" Hear the engine!

MAKING MAPLE SUGAR.

One warm spring morning
Father said, "Spring is here!
The sap will run to-day.
Come! We will tap the big maple trees."

"Oh! Oh! What fun!" said John and Mary.
"Here are the pails," said Father.

"We will carry them down to the maple trees."
Father made a hole in one of the trees.
He put a spout in the hole.
Then he hung a pail under the spout.
Soon the sap began to run out.
Drop by drop it ran into the pail.

"It looks like water," said John.
"It tastes like water with a little sugar in it," said Mary.

II

Father said, "I will tell you the story of the sap.
All winter the maple trees were asleep.
When spring came the warm rain ran down to the roots of the trees.
'Awake!' said the rain, 'It is time to grow.'
The bright sun looked down and said to the trees,
'Awake! It is time for the sap to run.'
Sap helps the little buds to grow.
In the spring the maple tree has more sap than it needs.
So we make a hole in the tree and the sap runs out.
Maple sugar is made from the sweet sap of the maple tree."

III

Near the maple trees there was a log house.
The next morning father made a hot fire in the log house.
"Now we will go to the trees and get the sap," said father.
He hung a big kettle over the fire.
They put the sap into this big kettle.
After a long time the sap was brown and thick.
"Here is some good maple syrup," said father.
He put the syrup into pans.
There were big pans and little pans and middle-sized pans.
"Here is a little pan for you, Mary.
This one is for you, John," said father.
"When the syrup is cold and hard it will be maple sugar."

THE WOODPECKER.

One day John was lying on the grass under a big maple tree.
All at once he heard some one tap on the tree.
"Tap, tip-y, tap, tap, tap! Tap, tip-y, tap, tap, tap!"
John looked all around.
Then he looked up in the tree.
He saw a woodpecker making a hole in the tree.
That is the way a woodpecker builds his nest.
Some chips fell on the grass beside John.
"Tap, tap!" went the busy little carpenter.
How happy he was at his work!

LITTLE GOODY TWOSHOES.

Once there was a little girl.
She was very poor.
She had but one old shoe.
A kind man gave her some new shoes.
Then the little girl was very happy.
She said to every one she met,
"See! Two shoes! Two shoes!"
So she was called Goody Twoshoes.

II

Goody Twoshoes could not go to school.
"I wish I could read," she said.
"I will ask the children to help me."
Every day she met the children when they came home from school.
They let Goody Twoshoes take their books.
Soon she could read better than her friends.
"Now I can teach other children to read," said Goody Twoshoes.
She made some letters out of wood.
She made nine sets of the small letters:—
a b c d e f g h i j k l m
n o p q r s t u v w x y z.
Then she made five sets of the large letters:—
A B C D E F G H I J K L M
N O P Q R S T U V W X Y Z.

III

Little Goody Twoshoes put the letters in a basket.
She first went to little Billy's house.
She knocked at the door, "Tap, tap, tap!"
"Who is there?"
"Little Goody Twoshoes," she said.
"I have come to teach Billy."
Little Billy ran to her and said,
"Good morning, Goody Twoshoes."
"Good morning, Billy," said little Twoshoes.

Goody Twoshoes put down the letters like this:—
b d f h k m o q s u w y z
a c e g i l n p r t v x j.
Billy picked them up and gave their names.
Then he put the letters like this:—
a b c d e f g h i j k l m
n o p q r s t u v w x y z.
Goody Twoshoes put down the large letters like this:—
B D F H K M O Q S
U W Y Z A C E G I
L N P R T V X J.
Billy picked them up and gave their names.
Then he put them like this:—
A B C D E F G H I J K L M
N O P Q R S T U V W X Y Z.

IV

Then she went to Sally's house.
Sally ran to her and said,
"Good morning, Goody Twoshoes.'
"Good morning, Sally," said Goody Twoshoes.
"Can you read for me?"
"Yes, I can read for you," she said.
Sally took the letters out of the basket.
Then she made words like this:—
Book, read, school, sing.
She made other words from the letters.
Then Goody Twoshoes went to other houses.
All the children were glad to see their little teacher.

THE BRAMBLE BUSH AND THE LAMBS.

A bright happy brook ran through a pleasant meadow.
The horses and cows and sheep went there to drink.
When the sheep and lambs went down to drink they passed by the bramble bush.
Sometimes the bramble bush would pick off little pieces of wool.
The sheep did not like this.
So they said to the bramble bush, "You are of no use.
We give the children wool to make warm clothes for the winter."
The cows said, "We give the children milk to drink."
The horses said, "We work for the children and give them pleasant rides."
But the bramble bush did not say a word.

II

One spring morning two pretty birds flew into a tree near the brook.
The sheep were eating the sweet green grass near by.
They heard a bird say,
"We must have something warm and soft for our nest.
I will see what I can find."
He flew down and saw the white wool on the bramble bush.
"This is what I want," said the bird.
"Thank you, Bramble Bush."
The bird took some of the wool to his nest.
Then he flew away to tell the other birds about the wool on the bramble bush.
After that the sheep were kind to Bramble Bush.
They often gave it wool for the birds to use in making their nests.

MARY'S LITTLE LAMB.

Mary had a little lamb,
Its fleece was white as snow;
And everywhere that Mary went
The lamb was sure to go.

It followed her to school one day,
Which was against the rule;
It made the children laugh and play,
To see a lamb at school.

So then the teacher turned it out,
But still it lingered near,
And waited patiently about
Till Mary did appear.

"What makes the lamb love Mary so?"
The eager children cry;
"Why, Mary loves the lamb, you know.'
The teacher did reply.
SARAH J. HALE.

SOMETHING TO TELL.

Was Mary's lamb white or black?
Where did the lamb go with Mary?
What did the children ask?
What did the teacher reply?
What did the children do?
What did the teacher do?
What did the lamb do?
What would you do if a lamb came to school?

Do you live in the city or the country?
Do you go to school?
What is your teacher's name?
Have you a book?
Can you read in it?
What book do you like best?
What story do you like best?

THE PET LAMB.

Lucy lives on a farm.
One day she and Father went to look at the sheep.
"Oh, Father!" she said. "What a pretty lamb! May I have him?"
"Yes!" said Father. "You may."
Lucy named him Lambkin.
Every day she came and fed him.
Lambkin loved her for she was kind to him.
He followed her all over the farm.
She did not like his dirty coat.
So Father washed Lambkin in the brook.
Now "its fleece was white as snow."
All summer Lambkin was Lucy's playmate. What fun they had!

II

The next spring Father said, "I must cut off Lambkin's wool.
He is too warm."
Lucy watched Father cut off the pretty white fleece.

"I wish I could have something made from Lambkin's wool," she said.
"I will make you some mittens," said Grandma.
Mother made the wool into soft yarn.
Then Grandma got her knitting needles and went to work at once.
How the needles flew!
So Lucy had her wish.
She had some warm mittens made from Lambkin's wool.

THE HOUSE IN THE WOOD.

A poor woodman lived in a little house near a great wood.
He had three little girls.
The oldest one did not like to work.
The second one did not do as she was told.
But the youngest girl was good and kind.
One morning the woodman went to work.
He said to the oldest little girl,
"Bring me my dinner to-day.
I will drop seeds along the path.
Then you can find the way."
When the sun was high the oldest girl went into the wood.
But she lost her way, for the birds had picked up all the seeds.
On and on she went until it was dark.
At last she came to a little house in the wood.
There was a light at the window.

II

She knocked at the door, "Tap, tap, tap!"
"Come in!" said a deep voice.
She went into the house.
An old man was sitting at a table.
Near him she saw a cock, a hen, and a spotted cow.
"May I stop here all night?" said the oldest girl.
The old man looked at the animals and said,
"Pretty cock,

Pretty hen,
And you spotted cow,
What say you now?"
"Yes," said the animals.
The oldest girl cooked a good supper.
Then she and the old man sat down at the table and ate it.
But she did not think of the poor animals.
After supper the animals said,
"You eat and you drink,
Of *us* you do not think.
So you shall have no bed,
To rest your tired head."
Then she had to find her way home alone through the dark wood.

III

The next morning the woodman went into the wood.
He said to the second little girl,
"Bring me my dinner to-day.
I will drop larger seeds along the path.
Then you can find the way."
At noon the second girl set out.
But the blackbirds had picked up all the seeds.
She went on and on through the wood.
At night she came to the little house in the wood.
"May I stop here all night?" said the second girl.
"I have lost my way."
The old man said,
"Pretty cock,
Pretty hen,
And you spotted cow,

What say you now?"
"Yes," said the animals.
The second girl cooked a good supper.
Then she sat down and ate and drank with the old man.
But the poor animals did not have any supper.
So they said,
"You eat and you drink,
Of *us* you do not think.
So you shall have no bed,
To rest your tired head."
Then she, too, had to find her way home alone through the dark wood.

IV

The next morning the woodman said to the youngest girl,
"Bring me my dinner to-day.
I will drop corn along the path.
Then you can find your way."
At noon the youngest girl went into the wood.
The doves had picked up the corn and she, too, lost her way.

At night she saw a light and came to the house in the wood.
"May I stop here all night?" she asked.
The old man said to the animals,
"Pretty cock,
Pretty hen,
And you spotted cow,
What say you now?"
"Yes," said the three.
The youngest girl went over to the animals and petted them.
She cooked a good supper for the old man.
But before she sat down to eat she gave the cow some hay.
Then she gave the cock and the hen some corn.
"Eat this, dear animals," she said.
"Then I will bring you some water."
After supper the animals said to the old man,
"She is kind and good.
Let her stay with us,
In the house in the wood."

V

Just then the youngest girl saw a bright light.
She covered her eyes.
When she looked up she was in a beautiful castle.
The old man was gone.
He was now a king's son.
The three animals had changed to three men.
"You were kind and good to my animals," said the king's son.
"So this is your castle."
Then the youngest girl sent for her father and sisters.
They all lived happily together in the beautiful castle.
JACOB AND WILLIAM GRIMM (ADAPTED).

THE LITTLE PLANT.

In my little garden bed
Raked so nicely over.
First the tiny seeds I sow.
Then with soft earth cover.

Shining down, the great round sun
Shines upon it often;
Little raindrops, pattering down,
Help the seeds to soften.

Then the little plant awakes!
Down the roots go creeping.
Up it lifts its little head
Through the brown earth peeping.

Higher and higher still it grows
Through the summer hours,
'Till some happy day the buds
Open into flowers.
EMILIE POULSSON.

WORK AND PLAY.

Once there was a little girl named Amy.
She liked to play in the garden and hear the birds sing.
She said the flowers and birds talked to her.
One day her mother said, "Amy, you are a large girl now.
You must help me a little.
Every day I will give you something to do."
"Oh Mother!" said Amy, "I do not like to work.
Please let me go into the woods and play."
"Yes," said her mother. "You may go and play.
I have no work for you to do just now."
So away Amy ran through the pleasant garden into the woods.

II

She saw a pretty squirrel and said,
"Dear squirrel, do you play and eat nuts all day long?
You do not work, do you?"
"Not work?" said the squirrel.
"Why, I am busy now.
I must put these nuts in my nest to eat next winter.
I can not stop to play with you."
Just then a bee flew by.
"Tell me, bee!" said Amy.
"Have you work to do?"

"Buzz! Buzz!" said the bee.
"I am busy now getting honey from the flowers.
I can not stop to play with you.
Amy walked through the woods.
By and by she met an ant with a piece of sugar.
"I wish you would come and play with me," said Amy.
"I am too busy to play with you," said the ant.
"I must carry this sugar home for the little ants to eat."

III

Amy sat down under a tree to think about it.
"The squirrels, the bees, and the ants work from morning till night," said Amy.
"I will ask the flowers if they have to work."
So she ran into the garden.
"Do flowers have to work?" she said to a pretty red clover.

"My dear Amy," said the red clover, "the flowers must all work.
We are busy now making honey for the bees.
That is why we are so happy."
Amy ran home to her mother and said, "I have come back to help you, Mother dear.
The squirrels, the bees, the ants and the flowers all have work to do.
I should like to work, too."
"You may help me sew," said her mother.
"Then you will be happy, like the squirrels, the bees, the ants, and the flowers."

THE THREE BROTHERS.

Once there were three brothers.
Not far from where they lived was the king's castle.
A large oak tree grew beside the door.
It made the castle very dark.
So the king said, "This tree must be cut down."
But no one could cut it down.
The more they cut the larger the tree grew.
The king's castle was on a high hill.
Every drop of water had to be carried up the hill.
So the king said, "I must have a well that will hold water all the year."
But no one could dig the well.
At last the king said, "I will give half my kingdom to the man who will cut down the tree and dig the well."

II

The three brothers set out to go to the king's castle.
On their way they passed through a great wood.
By and by they heard something chopping and cutting.
"I wonder what it is that is cutting and chopping," said the youngest brother.
"Did you never hear woodmen before? asked the brothers.
"Oh, yes!" said the youngest brother.
"But I should like to know what it is that we hear.
I am going to find out."
So away he went.
Far off in the woods he saw an ax chopping all alone.
"Good morning, Ax," he said.
"Are you cutting here all by yourself?"
"Yes," said the ax.
"I have been chopping here a hundred years, waiting for you.
"Well, here I am," said the youngest brother.
He put the ax in his bag.
Then he ran off to catch up with his brothers.

III

The three brothers walked on together.
By and by they came to a high hill.
They heard something picking and digging.
"I wonder what it is that is picking," said the youngest brother.
"Did you never hear a woodpecker before?" asked the brothers.
"Yes, I have," said the youngest brother.
But I should like to know what it is that we hear.
I am going to find out."
The brothers laughed at him, but away he went.
Far off in the wood he saw a pick digging all alone.
"Good morning, Pick," he said.
"Are you digging here all by yourself?
"Yes," said the pick.
"I have been picking here a hundred years, waiting for you."
"Well, here I am," said the youngest brother.
He put the pick in his bag.
Then he ran down to his brothers.

IV

On they went together until they came to a brook.
They sat down there to rest and to get a drink of water.
"I wonder where the brook comes from, said the youngest brother.
Well, did you never see a brook before?" asked the brothers.

"Yes," he said, "but I wonder where it comes from."
So he followed the brook.
At last he saw a tiny stream come out of a walnut.
"Good morning, Walnut," he said.
"Are you here all alone?"
"Yes," said the walnut.
"The water has been running here a hundred years, waiting for you."
"Here I am," said the youngest brother.
He put some moss in the hole in the walnut.
Then he put it in his bag.
"Did you find where the water came from?" asked the brothers.
"Yes," said the youngest brother.
"It came out of a hole."

V

The three brothers walked on until they came to the king's castle.
So many men had tried to cut down the tree that it was now very large.
At last the king said, "Every man who tries to cut the tree and can not do it must leave the country."
The oldest brother tried to cut down the tree.
But when the tree grew larger they sent him out of the country.
Then the second brother tried.
He could not do it, so they sent him out of the country.
"Now it is my turn," said the youngest brother.
He took his ax from the bag, and cut into the tree.

"My ax, cut for yourself," he said.
The ax chopped and chopped.
Soon the great oak tree fell down.
Then he took his pick from the bag.
"My pick, dig for yourself," he said.

You never saw such picking and digging.
Soon it had dug a great deep hole.
Next he took out his walnut.
He took the moss from the hole, then dropped the walnut far down into the well.
"Water, run," he said.
Soon the well was full of water.
The youngest brother had cut down the tree and dug the well.
The king gave him half of his kingdom.

THE LARK AND HER LITTLE ONES.

A lark built her nest in a field of wheat.
After a while there were five little larks in the nest.
One day the farmer and his son came into the field.
The farmer looked at the wheat and said, "This wheat is ripe.
It must be cut.
We will get our friends to come and help us."
"Oh, Mother!" said the little ones.
"The farmer says the wheat must be cut.
What shall we do?
We are not strong enough to fly."
"We need not fly away to-day," said the mother lark.
"But are you not afraid?" asked the little ones.
"No," said the mother lark.
"The farmer's friends will not cut his wheat."

II

In a day or two the farmer and his son came again to the field.
"Where are your friends?" said the farmer.
"This wheat is ripe. It must be cut."
But the farmer's friends did not come to help him.
At last the farmer said to his son,
"This wheat must be cut.
In the morning I will cut it myself.
You may help me, my son."
"Oh, Mother!" said the little ones,
"Must we fly away to-day?"
"Yes," said the mother lark.
"It is time for us to fly away.
In the morning the wheat will be cut."

MORNING SONG.

What does little birdie say,
In her nest at peep of day?
"Let me fly," says little birdie;
"Mother, let me fly away."
Birdie, rest a little longer,
Till the little wings are stronger.
So she rests a little longer,
Then she flies away.
What does little baby say,
In her bed at peep of day?
Baby says, like little birdie,
"Let me rise and fly away."
Baby, sleep a little longer,
Till the little limbs are stronger.
If she sleeps a little longer,
Baby, too, shall fly away.
ALFRED TENNYSON.

ALPHABET.

A	a	N	n
B	b	O	o
C	c	P	p
D	d	Q	q
E	e	R	r
F	f	S	s
G	g	T	t
H	h	U	u
I	i	V	v
J	j	W	w
K	k	X	x
L	l	Y	y
M	m	Z	z

WORD LIST.

THE following is a list of the words used in the First Reader, omitting those previously used in the Primer. They are grouped by pages, in the order in which they first occur.

5	apple
6	came
	waken
	kissed
	sang
	fell
7	doth
	shall
	himself
	hide
	head
8	blew

off

stronger

than

coat

9   now

very

soon

10   seen

neither

nor

leaves

hang

trembling

10   passing

through

	their
11	work
	does
	spring
	summer
	autumn
	winter
12	leaf-bud
13	sunshine
	dresses
	give
14	passed
	danced
	were
	covered

15	pine
	long
	needles
	wish
	should
	gold
	bag
17	happy
17	glass
	broken
18	goat
19	best
20	ant
	near
	dropped

21 shore

gun

tried

shoot

bit

foot

helped

23 brook

running

would

stay

boat

carry

heard

never

could

find

24 raindrops

sky

home

fishes

25 together

26 Golden Locks

bears

middle-sized

27 bowls

tasted

right

drank

28 chair

29 hard

bed

lay

31 voice

been

tasting

gone

sitting

32 lying

33 looking

jumped

34 fox

crow

cheese

must

	looked
35	falling
35	king
	met
	Henny Penny
37	last
	Cocky Locky
	Ducky Lucky
38	Turkey Lurkey
39	Foxy Loxy
	den
43	swing
	air
	think
	pleasantest

child

wall

till

wide

rivers

cattle

countryside

garden

roof

44 kind

old

oak

45 violets

afraid

47 woodmen

cutting

47 ax

logs

ice

melt

48 honest

large

chip

lifted

lost

fairy

lived

why

crying

50 silver

steel

52　mine

only

53　rhyme

great

axes

men

splash

54　seaside

beside

wooden

spade

dig

sandy

holes

empty

cup

more

55   Riding Hood

56   called

these

sick

path

57   wolf

59   pick

knocked

door

tap

60   cap

61   better

62   arms

      hug

      teeth

      killed

63   stream

      O

      pushed

      against

      wheel

      boards

64   zish

65   buzz

      busy

66   lion

66   paw

caught

let

please

67 net

him

cut

sharp

69 Browny

dirty

mud

Whitey

greedy

Blacky

70 cabbage

brick

	Mr.
71	carried
72	next
	eating
	knock
75	kettle
	back
	got
	rolled
76	full
	fire
	rolling
	ho
76	chimney
77	pitcher

handful

drop

began

cry

room

78   before

hope

she'll

any

79   I'd

nicely

sit

hold

both

ends

't would

beautiful

skies

clouds

roam

set

rise

rainbow

80 carpenter

81 sled

   mend

81 plane

   rap-a-tap

   hammer

   tick-a-tack

new

82 used

tools

83 gingerbread

woman

baking

84 oven

threshers

85 mowers

88 quarter

half

spoke

89 city

country

mice

	visit
	enough
90	while
93	bower
	friendly
	toads
	grudge
	seeds
	stalks
	timid
	furry
94	miner
	coal
95	dark
	lamp

click

click-ity

96   engine

puff

train

cars

97   maple

sugar

sap

pail

99   spout

hung

story

roots

100   awake

buds

needs

101 thick

syrup

pans

102 woodpecker

tip-y

builds

103 Goody

Twoshoes

104 school

read

children

books

nine

	small
105	five
	first
	Billy
	teach
107	picked
108	Sally
	words
	glad
	teacher
109	horses
	lambs
110	pieces
	use
	rides

111　about

　　　often

112　fleece

　　　sure

113　followed

　　　rule

　　　laugh

　　　still

113　lingered

　　　waited

　　　patiently

　　　appear

　　　eager

　　　reply

115　pet

Lucy

lambkin

loved

fed

washed

playmate

117   watched

mittens

yarn

knitting

118   oldest

119   second

youngest

bring

dinner

light

120　cock

spotted

121　animals

cooked

supper

table

rest

121　tired

alone

122　larger

125　petted

hay

126　castle

son

changed

127　sent

128　raked

tiny

sow

earth

cover

129　shining

shines

pattering

soften

peeping

higher

hours

open

130 Amy

liked

talked

131 bee

133 getting

133 honey

134 ask

clover

135 sew

136 brothers

well

year

138 kingdom

chopping

wonder

asked

139 yourself

hundred

waiting

140 walked

picking

digging

laughed

141 until

143 walnut

moss

144 tries

146 such

dug

147 lark

150 birdie

longer

flies

151 limbs